Governing in Excellence
How You Govern Your Business Determines Your Success

GWENDOLYN L. YOUNG

Copyright © 2014 Gwendolyn L. Young

All rights reserved.

ISBN:1494994690
ISBN-13: 978-1494994693

DEDICATION

This book is dedicated to my mother Jacqueline Barnes, who always told me I could be and do whatever I wanted to in life. I dedicate this book to her because she provided the platform for me to operate in my gift of administration and entrusted the operations and governance of her non-profit to my leadership. Thank you for your faith in me. I adore you more than you will ever know.

TABLE OF CONTENTS

DEDICATION iii

TABLE OF CONTENTS v

ACKNOWLEDGMENTS i

1 GOVERNANCE VERSUS MANAGEMENT 1

2 TWELVE PRINCIPLES OF EXCELLENT GOVERNANCE 5

3 FIVE CRITICAL GOVERNANCE POLICIES 9

4 THE TEN BASIC RESPONSIBILITIES OF ADVISORS 12

5 COMMON GOVERNANCE PITFALLS 14

6 THE IMPORTANCE OF STRATEGIC PLANNING 17

    The Strategic Planning Process 18

    Five Key Elements to Strategic Planning 19

    Executing the Strategic Plan 20

CONNECT WITH THE AUTHOR 22

ABOUT THE AUTHOR 23

ACKNOWLEDGMENTS

To my husband who loves me through everything, who understands and sacrifices his time with me so that I can author books, run foundations, and excel in my first love "business." Thank you for always supporting and encouraging me.

To my mentor Linda A. Cole who has set the example and been an exceptional role model of how women can be wives, mothers, great businesswomen and authors. She led by example and I am forever grateful for her being a part of my life.

To Lewis University, thank you for creating a culture of service throughout my graduate learning experience. It has given me the desire to govern better, to lead better, and to make a difference in my community.

1 GOVERNANCE VERSUS MANAGEMENT

Mark Goyder once said, "Governance and leadership are the yin and the yang of successful organizations. If you have leadership without governance you risk tyranny, fraud and personal fiefdoms. If you have governance without leadership you risk atrophy, bureaucracy and indifference." So, exactly what is governance?

Simply put, governance is the way an organization regulates itself. Governance ensures an organization takes the necessary precautions to protect itself, its employees, and its stakeholders from wrongdoing and unintentional harm; while strategically planning for the organization's future success. Governance has three critical elements: establishing strategic direction, executing organizational strategies and managing risks, and ensuring compliance with organizational policies.

Let's explore element number one: establishing strategic direction. Establishing strategic direction for an organization includes identifying the organization's vision, mission and core values. It includes defining the overarching goals of the organization and mapping out how an organization will do business. Why do we exist? Who will we serve? What need does our business, programs, and/or services fulfill? What do we want to accomplish? Where do we see ourselves in the future? Do our future goals align properly with our mission? How will we get there? These are the questions the governors, the advisors, and/or the board should be asking as they establish the strategic direction of the organization.

Element number one: establishing strategic direction is the single most important element of the governance process. Without strategic direction, an organization fails to authenticate its existence; thereby subjecting itself to misuse, exploitation, and manipulation. Dr. Myles Munroe once said, "When purpose is not known, abuse is inevitable." How can you effectively operate your business if you and/or the governors of your organization don't know and understand why it was created in the first place? Without strategic direction, your organization fails to market to the right audience, fails to engage the right stakeholders, and cannot establish proper procedures and operating policies.

Establishing strategic direction involves being able to objectively assess the organization; this is why having a governing body is critical to your organization's success. It involves asking tough questions such as, Do we have the right people in place? Are we managing our resources efficiently? Are the activities of the organization and/or ministry properly aligned with our vision and our mission?

It further protects the organization from founders syndrome, meaning all the decisions are based on a single person or single group of persons who have been with the organization for a lengthy timeframe rather than collectively and objectively as a whole. If an organization is reluctant to adapt to changing times and allow other decision-makers in on the process, their need to control will lead to the organization's failure and/or a continued repeated cycle of the same challenges with no growth.

The key to remember is that establishing strategic direction is the first element in the governance process and sets the overall organizational direction for the organization.

Without this element firmly established, none of the other parts of the organization or ministry can work cohesively together. Once the strategic direction for the organization has been identified, governors are responsible for introducing element number two: executing organizational strategies and managing risks.

Executing organizational strategies and managing risks is no easy feat. Execution requires skill, it requires a culture of accountability, and it requires an organization's human capital to change and/or adapt its behavior. This can be difficult in an organization and/or ministry that has no concrete goals or too many goals already at various levels of the organization. The key to execution is tri-fold, it involves: 1) the ability to focus on the most important goals 2) cascading that focus down to every level of the organization, and 3) implementing a framework of accountability.

The ability to focus on the most important goals can be difficult in day to day operations as urgent (not the most critical) issues arise, new ideas are generated, staff turnovers occur, new legislation is implemented, and community and/or client needs change. However, it remains critical that an organization integrate their goals into the culture of the organization. This can be done through internal company communications (i.e. newsletters, intranet sites, meeting agendas, etc.), employee training, new employee and volunteer orientation, and department meetings. Achieving this level of focus throughout an organization requires cascading the goals down to every level of the organization. This can be done through aligning organizational goals to individual employee performance reviews, management bonuses, and department goals. This is how the framework for accountability is created. Ensuring accountability is intertwined at every level of the organization helps to minimize risk.

Once element two has been deployed, the organization must effectively integrate element three; ensuring compliance with organizational policies and procedures. This will be key to minimizing risks for the organization. The organization can achieve success with this element by creating a culture of learning and required training. Training on policies and procedures can and should be done at the leadership levels; with requirements for department leaders to duplicate that training at the lower level within their departments for every employee. Excellent governance would include building an annual review of key policies and procedures into the performance management system. All three elements effectively executed ensures the organization has created a culture where the ability to focus on the most important goals exist, in addition to cascading that focus down to every level of the organization, and a solid framework of accountability throughout the organization.

This is governing in excellence; which serves as the master disaster catcher, increases your organization's creditability, and creates an atmosphere of transparency.

Management on the other hand focuses on the day to day operations of the organization; controlling, directing, staffing, organizing and planning. Management is making sure the strategies developed through the governance process are completed.

THE DIFFERENCE

GOVERNING	MANAGING
• Big Picture • Strategy • Building the framework for management • Overall responsibility for the work and actions of management	• Organizing the work • Doing the work • Day to day implementation of strategy

2 TWELVE PRINCIPLES OF EXCELLENT GOVERNANCE

Achieving excellent governance requires a conscious decision to be made at the top leadership level. An organization must genuinely want to operate from the highest level of governance, ensuring that it consistently looks toward the future while ensuring its current operation is ethical, stable, and cohesive at every level.

According to BoardSource, who was established in 1988 as the National Center for Nonprofit Boards by the Independent Sector and the Association of Governing Boards of Universities & Colleges, whose mission is dedicated to advancing the public good by building exceptional nonprofit boards and inspiring board service has identified twelve principles of excellent governance that power exceptional boards. These principles can be implemented across sectors and apply to governance as a whole. With permission from BoardSource to reprint and excerpt, we have listed the twelve principles below.

The twelve principles of governance include:

1. Constructive Partnership
    - Exceptional boards govern in constructive partnership with the chief executive, recognizing that the effectiveness of the board and chief executive is interdependent. They build this partnership through trust, candor, respect, and honest communication.

2. Mission Driven
    - Exceptional boards shape and uphold the mission, articulate a compelling vision, and ensure the congruence between decisions and organizational values. They treat questions of mission, vision, and core values not as exercises to be done once, but as statements of crucial importance to be drilled down and folded into deliberations.

3. Strategic Thinking
    - Exceptional boards allocate time to what matters most and ensure the congruence between decisions and core values.

4. Culture of Inquiry
    - Exceptional boards institutionalize a culture of inquiry, constructive debate, and engaged teamwork that leads to sound and shared decision making.

5. Independent-mindedness
    - Exceptional boards are independent-minded. When making decisions on behalf of the organization, board members put the interests of the organization above those of the chief executive, themselves, or other interested parties.

6. Ethos of Transparency
    - Exceptional boards promote an ethos of transparency and ethical behavior by ensuring that donors, stakeholders, and interested members of the public have access to appropriate and accurate information regarding finances and operations.

7. Compliance with Integrity
    - Exceptional boards govern with full recognition of the importance of their fiduciary responsibilities, developing a culture of compliance through appropriate mechanisms for active oversight.

8. Sustaining Resources
    - Exceptional boards ensure that the organization's resources are balanced with its strategic priorities and capacities. Individual board members extend the reach of the organization by actively using their own reputations and networks to secure funds, expertise, and access.

9. Results Oriented
    - Exceptional boards track the organization's advancement towards mission and evaluate the performance of major programs and services.

10. Intentional Board Practices
    - Exceptional boards make form follow function when it comes to their own operations. To provide stable leadership to the organization, they invest in structures and practices that transcend individuals and thoughtfully adjust them to suit changing circumstances.

11. Continuous Learning
    - Exceptional boards embrace the qualities of a continuous learning organization, evaluating their own performance and assessing the value that they add to the organization.

12. Revitalization
    - Exceptional boards revitalize themselves through planned turnover, thoughtful recruitment, and intentional cultivation of future officers.

Weaving these twelve principles into your governance process will put your organization and/or ministry on the path to success.

3 FIVE CRITICAL GOVERNANCE POLICIES

There are numerous policies an organization and/or ministry needs to have in place as it relates to operations. However, this resource will focus solely on the five critical governance policies every organization and/or ministry should have.

1. Conflict of Interest Policy
   - You can never avoid conflicts entirely, but you can take steps to prevent unjust enrichment to ensure that an insider, such as an advisor, leader, or staff person does not benefit from the transaction more than the organization.

2. Compensation Structure Policy
   - Compensation structures ensure that every individual hired into the organization is paid in a consistent and fair manner through the same pay structure. It further helps the organization to police itself and minimize risks as it relates to unfair pay practices.

- If your organization is a nonprofit, this policy is even more critical. The IRS requires a three-step process as it relates to compensation:
    - Review by an independent body
    - Use of comparability data
    - Documentation of how you arrived at the decision for pay practices

3. Media Spokesperson Policy
    - Every organization should have a clear policy on what happens when contacted by the media. It should be clear who is allowed to speak on behalf of your organization and how requests for interviews should be handled.

4. Public Disclosure Policy
    - Like the media spokesperson policy, it is equally important for every organization to know what documents they are required by law to provide upon public request. These documents should be easily accessible to staff along with education on how to respond to all requests.

    - For nonprofits, this is extremely important as it impacts your 501c3 certification with the IRS. Policies required by the IRS include:
        - Annual Returns (last 3 years) (all 990 schedules except schedule b)
        - Tax Exemption Letter
        - Articles of incorporation and all amendments
        - Bylaws and all amendments
        - Conflict of interest policy

- Form 1023 and all attachments; and
- Audited financial statements

5. Whistleblower
    - Implementing a whistleblower policy provides the organization an opportunity to respond and address unethical concerns brought to their attention. The whistleblower policy should encourage leaders and staff to report behavior, situations, etc. that are unethical and could potentially create a large risk for the organization.

4 THE TEN BASIC RESPONSIBILITIES OF ADVISORS

The board of advisors has ten specific responsibilities for governing the organization:

- Determine the Organization's Mission and Purpose
- Select the Executive Director
- Support the Executive Director and Review His/Her Performance
- Ensure Effective Organizational Planning
- Ensure Adequate Resources
- Manage Resources Effectively
- Determine and Monitor the Organization's Programs and Services
- Enhance the Organization's Public Image
- Serve as a Court of Appeal

The advisory governing board is always operating in three dimensions; fiduciary, strategic, and generative. The fiduciary mode is focused on good stewardship of the organization's assets, resources, and legal and fiscal compliance. Examples would include filing the appropriate state and federal returns, annual filing statements for the State, and/or ensuring grant monies are allocated to appropriate programs.

The strategic mode is ensuring the organization has a clear, focused, and specific strategic plan that aligns with the organization's mission. Examples would include hosting the strategic planning session, reviewing and modifying strategic plans, and monitoring performance against plans.

The generative mode focuses on identifying gaps and risk and thinking through solutions on how to address those gaps and risk. In this mode, the advisory board challenges organizational assumptions and ensures the organization's vision, mission, and core values are driving every decision of the organization.

It is important for boards to assess themselves and ensure they are operating effectively in all three modes; rather than one mode or none at all.

5 COMMON GOVERNANCE PITFALLS

There are ten pitfalls that organizational advisors should be aware of. They include:

1. Going in a direction that is not aligned with the mission
    a. This is particularly important when developing goals and/or new program and service offerings. All new programming and initiatives should be aligned properly with the mission of the organization.

2. Complacency
    a. The most tragic behavior your organizational advisors can engage in is complacency. When advisors are operating in this mode it stifles the growth and accountability of your organization.

3. Misguided Motivations
    a. Developing a board self-reflection and group reflection process can help to ensure that advisors are serving with the best intentions of the organization in mind; and not personal motivations.

4. Not establishing an elevator speech

a. It is critical that all advisors are representing the organization to the public in the same way. If there are multiple voices (advisors all saying something different about the organization) it can potentially discredit the work of the organization and confuse key stakeholders.

5. Micromanaging the CEO
   a. Micromanaging the CEO screams "we don't trust you!" The group of advisors are responsible for hiring and managing this individual's performance; therefore trust that you made the right decision in selecting this person. It is important for the relationship between advisors and CEO to remain strong; therefore; trust is a key element.

6. Not setting limits on advisory board terms
   a. Not setting limits for advisory board terms leads to pitfall number two "complacency." It is important for an organization to keep new blood pumping (new ideas, new perspectives, new people, and new engagement) through the veins of the organization. This requires actively preparing for succession of current advisory board members. The terms should be clearly spelled out in your organization's bylaws.

7. Unruly governance
   a. It is important that the advisory board specifically spells out in its organization's bylaws and/or conflict of interest policy how unruly governance issues will be handled. Organizations must remember that if the top leadership does not work cohesively and fails to govern itself; the impact will be felt throughout the entire culture of the organization.

8. Not assessing its own performance
   a. When the advisory board fails to assess its own performance, how can it know whether or not the group is successful and executing its responsibilities

effectively. Creating individual advisory board surveys in addition to a group advisory board survey will provide the opportunity for the advisory board to address any gaps, concerns, and challenges; as well as celebrate accomplishments.

9. Lack of self-improvement
    a. The advisory board should continuously look for opportunities to improve its knowledge and value to the organization. Failure to do so creates unruly governance.

10. Unwilling to invest
    a. It is highly recommended that the advisory board be 100% in giving to the organization. This can be done through establishing a minimum donation amount for each board member and/or a specific declaration that 100% giving is expected and allow board members to determine the level of giving they can comfortably afford.

    Tight purse strings from the top leadership of the organization provides a clear message to both staff and stakeholders that you don't value the organization enough to give yourself; so why should they be expected to invest.

6 THE IMPORTANCE OF STRATEGIC PLANNING

So what is strategy? Simply put, strategy is the roadmap you use to achieve your vision and reach your goals. The important thing to remember is that strategy cannot be developed until you have clearly defined your vision, mission, and values for the organization. So why is strategic planning an important part of the governance process? Because it does the following for your organization:

- Establishes long-term direction for the organization
- Establishes a framework for decision-making
- Sets the foundation for organizational planning
- Explains your business and/or ministry to others
- Serves as a catalyst for change

Additional benefits of strategic planning include:

- Personal satisfaction
- Forces the organization to think about its future position in the marketplace
- Provides a better understanding of the organization's current position and needs
- Creates a system of accountability throughout the organization

- Provides a tangible, workable, and realistic plan for achieving goals

So, what is the process and how do you get started? First, you must prepare to start the planning process. Preparation is key and involves the following:

- Identify Key Stakeholders who should be involved (i.e. leaders, employees, volunteers, etc.)
- Identify who will be the executive sponsor (generally board of directors and/or president/ceo if no board)
- Identify who will facilitate the session (internal vs. external consultant)
- Identify when and where the session will occur
- Begin with the END in MIND

Image adapted from Health Strategies & Solutions, Inc.

Four key questions that should be answered throughout the planning process:
- Where are we?
- Where do we want to be?
- How do we get there? (Close the gap)
- How do we evaluate our progress?

Five Key Elements to Strategic Planning

Environmental:
- SWOT (Strengths, Weaknesses, Opportunities, and Threats)
(internal: assets, resources, culture, partnerships, etc.)
(external: marketplace, competitors, target audience, technology, governmental rules/regulations)

Organizational Direction:
Are we mission driven? Meaning are our decisions, products, services, etc. guided by our mission and our values?
- If not, we need to reassess our mission

Strategy Formulation:
- What are the strategic issues we face? Those things that if we do not respond to will impact our growth, profitability, performance?
- This is where your strategic goals are created

Implementation:
- How do we get there?
- What tactics will we utilize?
- What key stakeholders need to be involved?

Evaluation
- How will we know that we achieved our goals? (Key Performance Indicators, action plans, plan report out)

Executing the Strategic Plan

- Plan should be future-focused
- Flexible
- Able to guide decision making at all levels of the organization
- Directly aligned with your vision, mission and values
- Goals and objectives should be clear
- Should be accepted by those who have to implement/execute
- Should identify timelines for progress report

Successful execution requires that the leadership continue to review the strategic plan, goals, and milestones to ensure adequate progress toward goal completion is being achieved. Do not let your strategic plan become a shelf plan.

"Corporate governance is not something that is put in place and then left. Ensuring its effectiveness depends on regular review, preferably regular independent review. And, in the end that comes down to the STAKEHOLDERS. Outside assessment and self-assessment need to be regular events." - Jim Jones (Business Day)

CONNECT WITH THE AUTHOR

E-mail: Gwendolyn@glyconsulting.com

Telephone: (224) 51-EXCEL

Web: www.glyconsulting.com

   www.facebook.com/glyconsulting

   @glyconsulting

For all speaking engagement requests, please complete the attached form and e-mail to Gwendolyn@glyconsulting.com

ABOUT THE AUTHOR

Gwendolyn L. Young is a certified professional coach. She received her Master of Art Degree in Organizational Leadership from Lewis University and graduated Cum Laude in undergrad from DeVry University. She is also a member of Sigma Beta Delta Business Honor Society.

Gwendolyn currently serves as Executive Director for Seed of Hope Foundation, a community non-profit in the western suburbs of the Chicagoland area. She has 15 years of business experience in operations and administrative management and serves as curriculum designer and workshop facilitator for Hope Center workshops. Gwendolyn has co-authored "20 Tips to Building a Strong Mother/Daughter Relationship," with her daughter Jacquelynne, in 2012 she received the Elizabeth Timpton Girls Mentoring Award for her work in the community by Passages Alternative Living, Inc., and was one of twenty emerging leaders in the United States selected as the recipient of the 2012, Judith O'Connor Scholar Award for Emerging Nonprofit Leaders by BoardSource.

Most recently, Gwendolyn was selected as a Stevie Awards preliminary round judge for Women in Business and honored as one of 2013's "Influential Women in Business," by the Daily Herald Business Ledger in partnership with the National Association of Women Business Owners — Chicago Chapter and the Women's Innovation Network. Gwendolyn sits on the Board of Directors for the African American Christian Foundation in Oak Park, Illinois to share her expertise and assist this organization with their growth strategy and governance challenges.

Most importantly, Gwendolyn is married to her love James A. Young of 17 years and a devoted mom of three young adult children. She is committed to excellence and has a strong passion for professionally developing young women.

www.ingramcontent.com/pod-product-compliance
Lightning Source LLC
Chambersburg PA
CBHW051828170526
45167CB00005B/2196